GEORGIAN GLUTEN-FREE AND LACTOSE-FREE RECIPES

FROM Helena

MEALS MADE SIMPLE

GEORGIAN GLUTEN-FREE AND LACTOSE-FREE RECIPES FROM HELENA

Photos: Nino Kankava and Goga Chanadiri
Edited by Katie Davies
Design by Ia Gabunia, Davina Bedwell
Cover Photo Location: L'Eclair de Génie Tbilisi
Editor assistants: Richard Eyre Vines, Bloomberg Chief Food Critic, Consultant Roland Debuyst Cook, 1997 Silver Bocuse "Bocuse d'Or Competition chez Bocuse d'Or Winners

Copyright © Helena Bedwell, 2021
All rights reserved.

For Betsy Haskell, neither gluten-free nor lactose-free, but supportive as only a real best friend can be!

INTRODUCTION BY ROLAND DEBUYST

As a professional chef, I'm amazed at and greatly admire Helena's work.

Helena is an incredible woman, who aims to bring her native Georgian cuisine to the front of the scene and at the service of everyone,,.

This cuisine, steeped in history and perfumes, I discovered in 2019 during my stay in Tbilisi. And Helena translated it perfectly into easy recipes, and even adapted it for people with certain intolerances.

The photos in this recipe book make me want to taste them all!

Dear Helena, I wish you good sales that will allow people to discover your beautiful country through beautiful gourmet recipes.

Bravo for another beautiful book!

Roland Debuyst

Executive Chef

Silver Bocuse 1997

1st Chef of Belgium "Prosper Montagné"

FOREWORD

Dear Readers,

I cannot believe this is my third book! It follows on from the debut of 'Georgian Flavours from Helena', which then led to 'Eat Georgian, Feel Good' for vegans and vegetarians.

When, for medical reasons, I was told to try gluten and lactose-free options, it began quite a journey for me. Gluten-free dishes come from all over the world, but I asked myself, what about Georgia?

So, I began experimenting in my kitchen, trying to adapt the wonderful Georgian cuisine to be gluten and lactose-free. I cannot say it was easy, but nor was it too difficult!

Thankfully, I have great family members and friends in Georgia and abroad to experiment on, but joking aside, yes, it is possible. Dedication and working on the techniques are key. When you have Georgian crown dishes, such as Khachapuri and Khinkali, made entirely of pastry and cheese, I thought, why exclude those that are intolerant to gluten and dairy foods? Let them enjoy my country's cuisine, too!

The truth is that I'm not a professional chef. I never graduated from a cookery school, nor have I owned a café-restaurant. Yes, I have taught a few cooking classes, but my knowledge comes from another, some say major, advantage: I am Georgian. More than that, I'm a Georgian woman who grew up seeing mum, dad, aunts, uncles and grandparents cooking, presenting, setting tables all year round to celebrate the seasons, special events or simply anyone coming through the door!

Georgian food is very hearty and is very like how the Georgian people are: emotional, straightforward and slightly over the top. Maybe you think there's too much on the Georgian table, or sometimes not enough, but no, it's always exactly what it should be.

That is the trait that has given this cuisine a special place in the hearts of many. It is sophisticated and yet simple. We won't argue that no other culture sets its tables quite like Georgia, that Black Sea country with glorious mountains, but where else would you hear the warmest, most inviting sounds from the Georgian wine cellar- the pouring of Orange wine into a clay vessel?

Families in cities and villages, strangers and friends alike, come, come, and join our Supra (feast), an event you will never forget. Being at the Georgian table is everything: it's a family tradition, a celebration of a birth, marriage, death, christening, or simply a guest popping round for no particular reason. The Georgian Supra is for everyone, and that is why my books are also for everyone: family-friendly and easy to follow.

Come, enjoy baking and cooking these Georgian gluten and lactose-free recipes with me! When the pandemic struck at the end of 2019, 2020 simply disappeared, like sand through our fingers, and my plans, like those of many, also changed. Despite the fact that I'm generally a super active person, working non-stop and creating, as well as entertaining friends from around the globe in my house or at my cooking classes, I didn't feel it was the time to write another cookbook. And yet, when I looked around and my heart ached for the declining economy, tourism, hospitality industry and people feeling desperate and down, I realised it was actually just the right time to write, because people needed to feel uplifted; to be encouraged to try something new.

I took the plunge and began jotting down recipes and twisting and changing them almost every day. I want to thank everyone who believed in this and helped me to create this totally unusual approach to what is usually very orthodox cuisine.

My team of Georgian chefs, restaurateurs, managers and brand creators believed in me and trusted me on this. More and more restaurants here are offering gluten and lactose-free options these days, and though most of these establishments are European, still, there is an ongoing hunger for something new.

I want to thank my beautiful photographer Emma Matevosyan, who took pictures for my two previous books, but who this time also recommended Nino Kankava to me, a talented young girl who tirelessly stood next to me in my kitchen while I prepared dishes, snapping away and wonderfully capturing their deliciousness every time.

ACKNOWLEDGEMENTS

My thanks also go to Goga Chanadiri, a dedicated patriot of his country and an awesome photographer who did not hesitate to take a wonderful cover picture for me!

As in my previous books, I used organic, home-grown products and good quality imports to achieve the best results. Gluten-free flours, good quality cornflours, fruits, vegetables, sun-dried fruits, nuts, lactose-free cheeses, spices, meats, and eggs: are all natural, boutique-style farmed, and carefully chosen.

Thank you, 'Barbale,' located in Atkusri, led and founded by Keti Didmanidze. Special thanks to the company 'Gastronomy' for providing the best duck breast for the 19th century recipe. Once again, thanks to the best Georgian brand of tea: Gurieli - born in Georgia -, and its chief Mikheil Chkuaseli. Many thanks to Gurieli for continuing Georgia's tea history and for featuring in this book!

This cookbook would also not have been possible without the help of marvellous young chef and restaurateur, Guram Kiknadze, originating from Abkhazia and an expert in its cuisine. Further thanks to Ana Tikaradze, a powerful vegan, gluten-and -lactose-free ideologist in Georgia, considering how unusual it is here, and to Meriko Gubeladze for sharing my excitement.

I want to thank all my colleagues - journalists, reporters and TV personalities in Georgia and abroad who helped me to promote my previous books, TV Mtavari and the amazing team, Nino Baratashvili, Nincho Jibladze, Tea Agladze, Giorgi Lapherashvili, Nino Darso, George Sharashidze, Maiko Tsereteli, Cate Popkhadze, Misha Robaqidze, Goderdzi Sharashia, the entire TV Pirveli team, Tako Gvazava, Sopho Megrelidze, CNN's remarkable Jill Doherty, Ellen Barry, Svenja O'Donnel, Wendell Steavenson, Pranvera Smith and her family, Rayhan and Robin, Lawrence Sheets, Matthew Collin for hanging around with me at the Frankfurt Book Fair, Nunu Japaridze, Molly Corso, my giant Bloomberg family, all loving my books, the

International Women's Association of Georgia with powerful ladies sharing my passion, Roy Southworth, who is no longer with us but forever in our hearts, and his wife Cathy Mclain, an unforgettable couple I was privileged to spend time with in Georgia, Sandra Roelofs, the former First Lady of Georgia, the large Sulakauri Publishing House team, especially Tina and Anna, Eka Sharashidze Voskamp and Gijs Voskamp, Tako Akhaladze, Lali Valois, Daro Sulakauri, Jana Sommerulnd, Marika Eliashvili, Yana Zakaidze, Nino Gorgiladze, Tata Sakhelashvili and everyone who appreciated what I do. Masha Levitov, Valeria Korchagina, Berdia Qamarauli, Agnes Lovasz, Peter Chilvers, Daniel Hamilton, the entire Emborg family, and all unknown customers who bought my cookbooks and wrote honest reviews!

Finally, I'd like to thank the Gastronaut Company, led by Lali Papashvili and Levan Qoqiashvili, and their handpicked team. Now they are parents, they'll undoubtedly be working even harder to make their country proud!

HELPFUL CONVERSIONS

My grandparents, aunt, mother and many Georgians use approximate ways to measure. Just a pinch, just a small dash, a little bit of, half a glass! And it can be just as hard for many Georgian chefs or home-cooks to say precisely how much time it takes to prepare a dish. We either work in the kitchen like a whirlwind or take our time. Starters should not take more than 15-20 minutes while the main dishes generally take about an hour to make.

This table should help you with measurements.

1 pinch = (dry) 0.5 gr
1 dash = 1.25 gr
1 teaspoon = (liquid) 5.0 gr
3 teaspoons = 1 tablespoon or 14.3 grams or ½ ounce
65 tablespoons = 1 pound or 453 gr
1 bunch of herbs = 45-55 grams
1 litre is 1.1 quarts

GAS MARK	FAHREBHEUT	CELSIUS	DESCRIPTION
1/4	225	110	Very cool/verry slow
1/2	250	130	---
1	275	140	cool
2	300	150	---
3	325	170	very moderate
4	350	180	moderate
5	375	190	---
6	400	200	moderately hot
7	425	220	hot
8	450	230	---
9	475	240	very hot

See other conversion charts on page 51.

NOTES ABOUT GLUTEN- AND LACTOSE-FREE OPTIONS IN THE GEORGIAN KITCHEN

Although a gluten-free diet is prescribed for those with celiac disease, there are also people like myself with gluten sensitivity: I suffered from bloating, stomach pain and irritability for some time. After serious thyroid surgery, my doctor suggested that a gluten-free diet could be beneficial for me, especially knowing the Georgian cuisine and its rich pastries. I'm also a vegetarian, and, due to my unconditional love for cheese, especially Georgian cheese, I decided not to go lactose-free. Still, I managed to successfully incorporate both lactose- and gluten-free cooking into Georgian cuisine.

Although sunflower oil is Georgia's favourite cooking oil, generally speaking, fats and oils are naturally gluten-free. That said, in some cases, additives that contain gluten may be mixed with fats and oils for flavour and thickening. So, read the labels and use them accordingly. Georgian recipes tend to work out fine with the following fats and oils:

1. Butter and ghee;
2. Olive oil, though not recommended for the Georgian cooking style, as it loses its flavor- sunflower oil is preferred;
3. Avocado oil;
4. Coconut oil;
5. Vegetable and seed oils, including sesame oil and canola oil.

Georgian's love wine and tea. Teas are gluten-free and healthy beverages, and here in this book, I offer you some lovely Georgian tea options, amazing when served with gluten and lactose-free desserts. However, some beverages are mixed with additives that contain gluten, and may contain malt, barley, or other such grains, and should be avoided when on a gluten-free diet.

1. Water;
2. 100% fruit juice;
3. Tea;
4. Some alcoholic beverages, including wine, hard ciders, and beer made from gluten-free grains, such as buckwheat or sorghum.

Georgian cuisine has spices, sauces, and condiments that often contain gluten, which can be overlooked. I haven't used store-bought packets here, unless labelled safe, instead making my own or buying the ingredients at the local market and blending them myself. Yes, spice blends can contain gluten, but you're almost always okay with individual spices and herbs. You'll need to go through your spice cabinet and check. Spices themselves don't contain gluten, just the processing or additives used.

Wheat-based sauces and malt vinegar should be avoided. Georgian salads normally use home-made malt vinegar, as well as apple cider vinegar, so look out for other safe options.

Varieties of spices are available to buy, such as blue fenugreek, yellow flower, Khmeli Suneli (Georgian spice mix at its best) and Svanetian Salt, but feel free to use any of your vegan-approved spices. Our yellow flower is called Imeretian Saffron, but is not comparable to the internationally known Saffron: It's marigold, which is calendula, also widely used abroad. So is Gitsruli, one of the main components of the Svanetian Salt mix, locally called "wild coriander". Old recipes also included cannabis seed, not widely used now, of course!

If you prepare Ajika (Georgian chili) sauce beforehand and store it in the fridge, then cooking will be easier: you can add it to any dish when cooking, as an alternative to spices and herbs. Lemon juice works as a condiment replacement too. Garlic and onions can be tricky, so omit them from the recipes if your body reacts to them.

Think Georgia, think Georgian cheese. When baking pastries, the varieties of cheese, among them Sulguni, Imeruli and Shebolili (smoked), are what comes to mind. I know many of us who react to gluten and lactose tend to be picky about cheeses. Goat's cheese is most tolerable, but it's not ideal for baking. The Georgian cheeses above, or sheep's cheese, are the lowest in lactose. Georgia does have a history of goat and sheep cheese making, but it is normally consumed as it is, rather than baked or boiled. Vegan cheese is made from nuts and vinegar, and many have issues with that. Gluten-free people can happily consume Swiss, havarti, Parmesan, cream cheese, and mozzarella, as well as non-dairy cheeses. In this cookbook, I opted for some nice brands that worked for me, such as Violife, but please feel free to make the choice that works best for you.

If you're avoiding gluten, there are still plenty of foods to choose from, although many Georgian foods are naturally gluten- and lactose-free, including fruits, vegetables, legumes, certain whole grains and oils, as well as fresh meat, fish, and poultry.

And because gluten is also commonly added to processed foods, such as canned and boxed items, we don't use them in my book.

It is super important to concentrate on your ideal flour mix. Yes, there are many available to buy, but if you're making one yourself, why not experiment a little? In most of my recipes, I've used an all-purpose flour blend that is 100% gluten-free.

One of my great readers from Canada told me that her family's ideal recipe called for 2 cups of white rice flour, 1 cup of tapioca flour (also called tapioca starch), and 1 cup of potato starch. Mix them together well in a large bowl, then store in a large airtight glass bottle. The flour blend can be stored in a cupboard for up to 1 month this way, and for longer-term storage, keep it in the refrigerator. As for the binder, I use 1/2 teaspoon of xanthan gum per cup of flour blend.

Ensure your kitchen is completely gluten-free, and if you have to share the kitchen, you need to be super careful. Many people are allergic, others are gluten-free by choice. Let's respect that.

Eggs, mushrooms, and nuts all feature in my cookbook, but you may want to replace them. It really depends on the recipe. For example, to get the result I want, sometimes I find it best to use eggs, but eggs can be replaced with apple sauce, banana, ground flaxseed, tofu or soy yoghurt. I've tried them all successfully in baking; and in all my vegan dishes, I naturally use an egg substitute.

First of all, let's learn how to make Mchadis. You can make them whatever shape you want: round or diamond, flat or thick, fried, or on a large baking tray.

Mchadi, Georgian cornbread, is one of my favourite, if not my most favourite item on the Georgian table. Not only is it an amazing gluten-free alternative to serve with starters or main dishes instead of wheat bread, it's also healthy, tasty and is what distinguishes Georgia from other cuisines that use maize flour in the kitchen.
Diamond-Shape and Round Mchadis

FIRST COURSES
AND LIGHT DISHES

HOW TO MAKE

Take the cornflour, add a pinch of salt and then the boiled water and stir carefully until you get the consistency of playdough. Add a drizzle of oil and some baking powder. Make diamond shapes or rounds from the mix and put them either in the oven or pan-fry them. Meriko Gubeladze, one of my favourite chefs in Georgia, recommends you pre-roast the cornflour, mixing it with water; you will get slightly browned Mchadi with a smoky flavour. I found that, according to the 19th-century recipe cookbook by Barbare Jorjadze, mixing the flour with boiled water instead of lukewarm or even cold water is much better, as it softens the flour.

When the Mchadis are ready, allow them to cool down and then cut in the middle sideways. Put the medium sliced gluten-free cheese selections of your choice inside or spread on Georgian Pkhali, as shown in the picture. Read on for the recipes.

INGREDIENTS:

200g Maseca flour
200g water
1 pinch of salt
A little oil
Gluten free baking powder optional

MCHADI SANDWICHES WITH MKHALI SELECTION

HOW TO MAKE

You'll need a good blender to make this one, as the old pestle-and-mortar way would take a long time. Combine the walnuts, garlic and spices along with vinegar and water to make the walnut paste. Blend well until you get a nice thick yellowish paste with a beautiful aroma.

From each large aubergine, you should be able to get 4-5 long flat slices. In Georgia, to make aubergine dishes, they first sprinkle the slices with salt, or you can also fry the slices directly in oil over a medium heat.* Make sure they have browned well before turning.

Place the fried slices on kitchen paper to absorb the extra oil, then put them on a flat wooden board and wait until they have cooled before spreading them with the paste. Roll them gently into parcels. Serve chilled and eat as-is, or put them inside a Mchadi sandwich!

* I find that baking aubergines in the oven is also an excellent method, and the slices come out drier.

INGREDIENTS:

500g large aubergines
250g walnuts
2 cloves of garlic
2 tbsp sunflower oil parsley1 tsp dry coriander
1 tsp of chili (fresh or dry)
1 tsp of blue fenugreek
1 tsp marigold3 tbsp vinegar
Salt to taste
Pomegranate seeds
A handful of fresh herbs to garnish, such as parsley

WALNUT AUBERGINE PARCELS

HOW TO MAKE

Both pumpkin and butternut squash are ideal for this starter. It's a great festive, colourful dish to serve in any season, and tasty too!

Bring a large pan of water to the boil. Reduce the heat and put the chopped and skinned pumpkin or butternut squash pieces into the pan. Boil until tender. Poke them with a fork from time to time, as we will be pureeing the pieces anyway. Alternatively, bake them before pressing.

Meanwhile, make the paste in the food processor, mixing all the spices and walnuts. Making the paste will require about 5 minutes because the paste must be smooth and not chunky. I find adding a bit of boiled water also helps to get the paste to the right consistency.

Take the boiled pieces of pumpkin or butternut squash and mash them with a fork. Do not blend in the food processor because they needs to have a stringy appearance. Now mix all the ingredients and garnish them with pomegranate seeds or herbs.

I find this dish tasty served both warm and cold.

INGREDIENTS:

1 kg fresh pumpkin or butternut squash
200g chopped walnuts or almonds
3 cloves of garlic1 tsp chili (fresh or dry)
Dry herbs, such as coriander or parsley (fresh or dry)1 tbsp dried marigold
3 tbsp of vinegar
Salt to taste
Pomegranate seeds and herbs to garnishA few tbsp of sunflower oil

PUMPKIN PKHALI

HOW TO MAKE

Take a medium saucepan half-filled with water. Heat until it starts to boil, then put in 1 cup of beetroot leaves. Allow the greens to remain in the boiling water for about 5 minutes. Take out the leaves and wait until they become totally dry, then chop finely.

When the leaves are prepared, mix the walnuts, salt, pepper, garlic, coriander and blue fenugreek. Add vinegar and a little bit of leftover boiled water. Add the chopped onions and mix well.

Now add the mixture to the chopped leaves and mix well by hand. Make small balls in the shape of a bird's nest and place a few pomegranate seeds inside.

The ready Pkhali can also be garnished with marinated beetroot balls.

INGREDIENTS:

1 kg beetroot leaves
250g walnuts
2 large onions
1 tsp of ground corianderA handful of coriander seeds
Salt and pepper
2 tbsp red vinegar½ tsp blue fenugreek
One or two small marinated beetroots

BEETROOT PKHALI

INGREDIENTS:

1 kg fresh spinach or shard*
200g chopped walnuts
3 cloves of garlic
3 onions, choppedA few tbsps of sunflower oil
1 tsp blue fenugreek
1 tsp chili (fresh or dry)
1 tbsp marigold1 tsp of dry coriander
3 tbsp vinegar
Salt to taste
Pomegranate seeds to garnish
How to Make

HOW TO MAKE

Bring a large pan of water to the boil and add the spinach. Cook for a minute or so until it softens. When ready, drain it in a colander and set it aside until it is cool enough for you to handle.

When ready, take snowball-sized handfuls and squeeze hard to remove the excess water. Chop the drained plant finely and leave it to settle while we make the walnut paste.

The paste is made in the same way as previously described, in a food processor. Mix slowly, adding all the remaining ingredients. You can sauté the onions (or if you like spring onions) separately in oil and set aside for later.

Take the chopped spinach and combine well with the walnut paste, mixing by hand. Adjust the consistency to taste. Add the sautéed onions and serve either as small balls or lay flat on a beautiful serving plate, garnishing with the pomegranate seeds.

* Both chard and spinach, and even leeks, are suitable for this kind of green starter. My grandmother also used nettle. Of course, it is up to you to show off your imagination and use the greens of your choice. The secret is to get stuck in with your hands when making this Pkhali, as it requires a lot of playing around to get the flavours fully absorbed!

Note: The vegetables in these recipes can be replaced with vegetables of your choice, such as string-beans, leeks, onions and carrots- the sky's the limit! 15 minutes is the approximate time you would need to make it.

SPINACH PKHALI

HEARTY SALADS

HOW TO MAKE

This salad is Georgia's trademark. It's a simple but deliciously flavoured salad, easy to make, easy to serve, and a delight for vegetarians. Walnuts give an extra boost, but nut allergy sufferers can cut this ingredient out.

Cut the cucumbers and tomatoes into pieces. You can peel the cucumbers if you like. It's best to mix the ingredients by hand, slowly adding the seasonings.

Serve chilled.

* This salad is also served without adding walnuts and with more sunflower oil and vinegar. In this book, the salad is shown served with Mchadi sandwiches. See page 18?

INGREDIENTS:

1-2 long cucumbers
6 small or 3 large tomatoes
1 large onion
Fresh herbs of your choice1 tbsp of thick sunflower oil
A drizzle of vinegar
A handful of crushed or chopped walnuts*Salt and pepper

GEORGIAN STAPLE SALAD

SPINACH, CUCUMBER AND WALNUT SALAD

INGREDIENTS:

Bunch of fresh spinach
2 cucumbers
1 red onion
Crushed walnuts

HOW TO MAKE

Cut the cucumbers into round shapes. Lightly sauté the spinach in oil, add the salt and pepper, and place it on the salad plate. Add the cucumbers and onion cut into rings, and sprinkle with the walnuts.

PEELED TOMATO AND LACTOSE-FREE CHEESE SALAD

INGREDIENTS:

3 large tomatoes, skinned
Lactose-free cheese of your choice
1 onion
Apple cider vinegar
Oil of your choice
Fresh parsley leaves
Salt and pepper to taste

HOW TO MAKE

Peel the tomatoes and cut them into round or wedge shapes. Cut the onions as rings and toss with the tomatoes, adding the oil, vinegar and herbs. Serve and add the lactose-free cheese of your choice. Top it with more parsley leaves.

HOT STARTERS

HOW TO MAKE

Cut the aubergines into long slices. Place the chopped pieces in a bowl and sprinkle them with salt. This will allow the aubergines to release any extra moisture so they won't get overcooked or absorb too much oil. Leave to stand for at least 30 minutes.

Fry the onions in the oil until lightly browned. Add aubergines and potatoes (which have been soaked in boiling salty water to release extra starch).

Continue to simmer, slowly adding all the remaining ingredients, until the vegetables are nicely mixed and softened.

Add tomatoes, fresh and then tinned, cover, and continue to simmer. Stir slowly. Add salt and pepper and any other herb/spice you find interesting. Be creative!

Georgians love to serve this dish cold, but hot is fine. Before serving, sprinkle with hand-chopped fresh herbs. Enjoy!

* You can add any other vegetable you like. I also add cauliflower, which works well with the rest of the colours.

INGREDIENTS:

500-600g aubergines

4-5 onions

Handfuls of herbs such as coriander, parsley or basil

5 carrots

5 fresh tomatoes

4-5 peppers (sweet or chopped)

Tinned tomatoes (chopped or puree)

4 cloves of garlic

4-5 potatoes (sweet or regular)

500 g Green beans

One small red chili

Salt and pepper to taste

AJAFSANDALI
RATATOUILLE, GEORGIAN STYLE

VEGETABLE MTSVADIS

Normally, Georgians would use red meat pieces, spit-roasted on the barbeque grill, but vegetables are much healthier, more colourful and just as enjoyable. There's enough in this recipe to make a good meal for 3.-4 people. Use any vegetables of your choice and use the leftovers for the next day to make sandwiches.

INGREDIENTS:

6 tbsp of oil of your choice
Juice of half a lemon
Salt and pepper
1 aubergine, cut into rounds
2 small onions, cut into thick rings
2 large tomatoes, sliced
Green, red and yellow sweet peppers (1 of each)

HOW TO MAKE

Cut all ingredients into the desired shapes, larger is better, then in a large bowl combine them all with the oil, lemon juice, salt and pepper. Garlic is optional.

Let it soak a bit before arranging them on wooden spits. Alternatively, you can place them under the oven grill.

Turn the vegetables over from time to time, cooking for about five minutes. Don't worry if they burn lightly, as long as they are not charcoaled! Serve them warm.

Best served with nice gluten-free flat-bread and sauce.

If you have a nice clay baking dish, use that. If not, an ordinary one will do. Mushrooms are a very important part of the Georgian cuisine, connected to the historical way Georgians used to eat. Mushroom picking and preparation for a variety of dishes is a piece of very important knowledge, plus they are an ideal replacement for meat and equally beneficial for gluten-free dieters. The dishes here are served with Mini Shoti breads

Apart from the specific shape, simply use the bread dough of your choice and give them this specific shape to copy the famous Georgian shoti bread. Bake them till brown on top, and brush with oil and herbs.

If you thinly flatten the dough, you can also get Georgian Khmiadi, think flatbreads, served browned and crispy. See photo on page 38.

HOT DISHES ON KETSI

SWEET POTATO DISH WITH TKEMALI

INGREDIENTS:

3 large sweet potatoes
Salt and black pepper
Several tbsp. of cooking oil of your choice
Tkemali to garnish

HOW TO MAKE

Wash, peel and dry the sweet potatoes. Pre-boil them in salty oily water until tender, then place them on the clay baking dish and put them under the grill. You may add extra oil to the baking dish. When the potatoes are slightly crusted and appear ready, take them out of the oven and leave them to set, but not cool down. Pour Tkemali sauce or any other sauce of your choice around it, so the potatoes are like a small island in the middle.

*In this picture we used the green Tkemali recipe.

MUSHROOM CHASHUSHULI

INGREDIENTS:

500g of any kind of mushrooms
1 onion
2-3 cloves of garlic
3 tbsp oil of your choice
One small bunch of spring onions
One small bunch of tarragon, parsley and coriander (fresh)
Salt and pepper to taste

HOW TO MAKE

Wash the mushrooms well, cut them to the desired size and sauté them on a low heat until the juices are released. If the water evaporates easily, add some more.

When the water is gone, add oil and chopped onions with garlic. Allow to simmer some more, stirring occasionally.

Chop all the green herb ingredients, add, and cook a further 10 minutes. Season with salt and pepper, and enjoy!

INGREDIENTS:

400.g button mushrooms
1.g Georgian Sulguni cheese, lactose-free mozzarella, or any kind of stretchy cheese
50g butter or oil of your choice
Salt to taste

HOW TO MAKE

Wash and prepare the mushrooms, removing the stalks.

Place the mushrooms upside down, so the inside of the mushroom is facing upwards. Sprinkle with salt and add a cube of butter to each or drizzle with oil and the cheese.

Pre-heat the clay ketsi in the preheated oven at 250C. Place the mushrooms in the dish and cook until the cheese is well browned. You'll know it's ready when the melted cheese stretches when you pick up a mushroom!

MUSHROOM KETSI WITH CHEESE

Another very Georgian dish, favoured by many as a morning freshener after a heavy day/evening before. It's also a great pick-me-upper when you're feeling under the weather.
Every time I feel under the weather, my mum makes me this soup. Green apples are a meaty and juicy replacement for potatoes. A plethora of vegetables and the aroma of green apples makes for a perfect heart-warming soup.

SOUPS

CHIKHIRTMA SOUP

INGREDIENTS:

- 1 chicken
- 5 eggs
- 2 onions
- 4 cloves garlic
- 100g butter
- 1 tbsp vinegar
- 2 tbsp gluten-free flour mix
- 2 bunches coriander
- 1 bunch dill
- Salt, black pepper to taste

HOW TO MAKE

Boil the chicken in salty water. When ready, take the chicken out and let it set, sprinkle with some additional salt if you like. Drain the chicken stock through a fine strainer and then add pre-sauteed onions and two tablespoons of gluten-free flour, pre-blended with some water.

Let it boil well and blend in three whisked eggs. Add vinegar and keep whisking until you get a nice consistency.

Add coriander, cut the pre-boiled chicken into your desired pieces and serve the soup with a single piece of chicken in each bowl, sprinkled with dill. Garlic is optional.

MY MOTHER'S GREEN APPLE SOUP

INGREDIENTS:

- 1 large onion
- 3 green apples
- 2-4 sweet peppers cut thinly
- 1 small cup of fresh corn (optional)*
- 100g wild rice
- 1 large head of broccoli
- 1 cup of string beans
- Oil of your choice and some water

HOW TO MAKE

In a large saucepan, sauté the onions lightly in oil.

Add the wild rice and keep stirring until the onions are brown. Add the vegetables, chopped apples and continue to simmer.

Finally, add water, and salt and 2-4 sweet peppers, cut thinly to taste. Fresh or dry herbs are optional.

*Since many react to sweetcorn (though I do not) I have decided to leave this up to you and make the corn optional.

MAINS

Bajhe is a walnut sauce, and it goes with any kind of dish, be it poultry or vegetables, though it goes best with Georgian polenta, as shown in the picture. This time, we're going to try it with fish. It's a true discovery.

INGREDIENTS:

2 pieces of salmon fillet, 150g each
150g walnuts
Red chili
4 cloves of garlic
10g blue fenugreek
10g dry coriander
5g marigold
Salt to taste
300 ml water, pre-boiled

GRILLED SALMON IN BAJHE

HOW TO MAKE

First prepare the fish. For the gluten-free option, make sure you buy local and check the label. Set the grill to high and allow at least 5 minutes on each side, then sprinkle with salt on each side and serve with the walnut sauce. Alternatively, fry the fish.

You'll need a good blender for this sauce. Mix all the ingredients and add salt at the end, and chili if desired. Slowly add stock or water while stirring by hand or continuing to blend. Watch the consistency. You should be able to get a thick paste, which can be blended again, adding a teaspoon of warmed vinegar or pomegranate juice. I recommend using a wooden spoon when stirring by hand.

Make sure you use mature garlic for this and not fresh.

For fish, add more coriander. Pour the sauce over the fish or dip the fillets into the sauce deeply.

*try ground almonds instead of walnuts.

This dish, a version of polenta, is a Georgian delight and ideal if you want a quick-carb fix. Make sure you prepare it inside a cast-iron pot to get the best results.

Normally, Georgians mix it with cheese, but as a vegan option, it goes ideally with any of the sauces mentioned in this book or your sauce of choice. Also, one of the best versions I came across was with crushed walnuts, some chili or lactose-free cottage cheese.

INGREDIENTS:

300g ghergili (coarse maize flour)
1 litre of water to make a simple polenta

HOW TO MAKE

Simply mix both ingredients and place them in a pan over a medium heat, stirring constantly until it starts to thicken. Leave to cook, further stirring from time to time until the smell of flour disappears and the grains are soft. It will probably take around 90 minutes. Serve as a side dish. See pic on page?

GHOMI, GEORGIAN POLENTA

WEIGHT	
OUNCES	GRAMS
1	25
2	50
3	75
4	110
5	150
6	175
7	200
8	225
9	250
10	275
11	315
12	350
13	365
15	400
15	425
1b	450

WEIGHT	
FLUID OUNCES	MILLILITRES
1	25
2	55
3	75
4	120
5	160
6	175
7	200
8	225
9	250
10	274
15	425
pit1	570
125	725
1.5	850
1.75	1 litre

This dish is normally made with beef, but I have recreated it using mushrooms and chicken. You can also use courgettes or aubergines, substituting them for mushrooms. Kharcho normally includes walnuts, but ground almonds are far better alternatives, and you should definitely give them a try!

INGREDIENTS:

1 onion, sliced into rings
1 large chicken, chopped
400g ground almonds
2 tsp blue fenugreek
1 tsp dry coriander
Half tsp yellow flower (Imeretian Saffron)
1 tbsp red ajika
1 large pomegranate
1 bunch of fresh parsley
Salt and pepper and 2-3 cloves of garlic to taste

CHICKEN ALMOND KHARCHO

HOW TO MAKE

Preheat the oil in a saucepan. Add the chicken and onion and cook until the chicken is tender and has released its fats. If it isn't fatty, add oil of your choice or butter. My grandmother used to add a touch of tomato paste.

Add enough water to cover the chicken and allow it to cook completely.

When ready, add 3 cups of ground almonds, crushed garlic, chili or the Georgian Ajika, and all additional spices. Allow to cook for 15 more minutes and then drop in a fresh bunch of parsley secured with string. Take the herbs out when the dish is ready. Add salt.

*This dish is ideal served with Georgian polenta or with your choice of side dish.

This chicken is aromatic and is prepared in a special way, flat-fried, and best served with cold vegetable salads, as the chicken is spiced with Ajika sauce (see the Ajika recipe). That said, you can easily tone down the spice if you wish.

My grandmother used to cut the chicken from the back and flatten it to prevent the chicken breast over-drying while frying.

INGREDIENTS:

1 whole chicken
90g butter or cooking oil of your choice
Salt and pepper
1 tsp dried coriander seeds
2 tsp paprika
4-5 tbsp apple cider vinegar
Several cloves of garlic
Ajika paste

CHICKEN TABAKA WITH AJIKA

HOW TO MAKE

Cut the chicken from the back and flatten. You can use a meat tenderizer to flatten it further.

Rub it well with garlic-infused vinegar and let it soak. Set aside. Garlic is optional, as we'll be using Ajika sauce.

Mix salt, pepper, paprika and ground coriander seeds and rub over the pre-soaked chicken (both sides).

Put the frying pan on the stove, melt the butter or cooking oil, put the chicken in, and cover. You can weigh the chicken down by using a heavy stone pestle, for example. Continue to fry until the chicken is a lovely brown colour and crispy, then turn it over and repeat.

When the skin is crispy all over, remove the stone and continue frying. Place the chicken on a large serving dish and allow it to cool down a bit before smothering it well with Ajika.

Serve as whole or as shown in the picture, cut into pieces.

One of my favourite women, Barbare Jorjadze, had this in her 19th century Georgian cookbook. I decided to try it out for my family, adding blackberries. It's a simple, yet very glamorous dish made with tender duck breasts.

INGREDIENTS:

1 duck breast
Anise flower
1 kg of blackberries and cornelian cherries
Butter or ghee
Salt and pepper

HOW TO MAKE

I did not marinate the breasts, as the dish itself is quite juicy. There are a few ways to fry the perfect duck, and I chose the frying pan, which melts the fat and helps the skin to crisp up without it burning.

Fry the breasts, letting the fat melt out and the skin crisp. This can take up to 15 minutes.

Make the sauce by mixing all the berries together. Sauté with anise flower, salt and pepper, and pour the mixture over the duck breast. You're done. Enjoy!

*Thank you Gastronomy shop in Georgia, Tbilisi for providing the duck breast for this recipe.

DUCK BREASTS WITH CORNELIAN CHERRY, BLACKBERRIES AND ANISE FLOWER

Meats, vegetables or eggs in Georgian Tkemali, or simply berry sauce alone, are amazing. My grandmother used to fix a quick late lunch for her friends, or for those field workers helping her harvest her orchard, with simple proteins like chicken pieces, boiled eggs, or veggies dipped in tangy sauces: cold and refreshing on hot sunny days!

Red Berry Sauce
Use red berries of your choice; I chose red gooseberries, currants, and red berries. Lightly sauté the berries with some water, salt and pepper.
Slowly add dry herbs of your choice, and fresh, crushed coriander. Garlic is also an option. Blend it well until you get a thick consistency.

You can use this sauce served with chopped chicken pieces, boiled or fried.

Alternatively, use hard boil eggs and dip them in the sauce. My tip is to let them sit in the sauce a while to absorb the flavours to the maximum.

Cauliflower is another ideal partner for this sauce. The combination of red and white is beautiful, and meaty cauliflower chunks are perfect for vegans and vegetarians.

RED BERRY SAUCE PLATTER

Georgian sweet Plavi is normally served at ritual tables, such as at funerals and New Year's celebrations. It's certainly a dish which has been adopted from our neighboring cuisines, but still, my aunt Medea's recipe is my all-time favorite, with dried fruits and nuts drizzled with oils. And since brown and wild rice are the best gluten-free options, I have opted for them. Served best with sweet boiled fruit, called Muraba. In the picture, you'll see it served with baby acorn Muraba.

INGREDIENTS:

500g mixed rice, brown and wild
1 lemon
200g lactose-free butter or coconut oil
1 packet of vanilla or a vanilla stick
3-4 tbsp dried fruits and nuts, chopped
4 tsps honey or agave nectar
Salt to taste
Cinnamon or other spices to taste

BROWN AND WILD RICE SWEET PLAVI

HOW TO MAKE

I know it's a very tricky subject, how to cook rice. Here, you can simply use the method that suits you best. Use a heavy-based pan, cast iron is ideal.

First pre-soak the rice for several hours, drain and rinse, then bring a large pan of salty water to the boil and add the rice. Simmer for at least 5-10 minutes, then rince and set aside. The rice must be fluffy and separated.

Melt the butter or coconut oil in the pan. My aunt used to put half an onion in the oil to difuse the flavours, but this method is more for when you'll only be adding raisins to the dish. Since we'll be using many other dried fruits and nuts here, it's better to use only the butter or coconut oil.

Put all the nuts and dried fruits in the pan and simmer well before adding cinnamon, vanilla, lemon juice or fruit slices. Make sure the mixture doesn't stick to the pan.

Add the cooked rice and mix well, or pour the ingredients from the pan into the bowl of rice and mix well. Note, we didn't use any sugar, since most of the sweetness will come from the dried fruits and nuts sauteed in sweet syrup.

Beans (lobio) is one of the most authentic and memorable dishes for those visiting Georgia. Although beans were not thought to have come initially from ancient Georgia, as I was writing this book, a discovery was made proving that Kolkhuri wild beans were grown and consumed by our ancestors.
Nevertheless, the way we cook bean dishes today is unlike anything you'll find elsewhere in the world. With or without walnuts or almonds, it's a dish packed with proteins!

BEANS

LOBIO, BLENDED

INGREDIENTS:

1 kg red kidney beans

A bunch of fresh coriander

3 cloves of garlic

Beans (canned ones can be used)

1 tsp savory

3 large onions

Salt and pepper to taste

A bit of tomato paste

HOW TO MAKE

If using dry beans, pre-soak them the night before. Boil the beans but pour out the water the first time it boils, then add more water and continue to simmer. When making Lobio, which is a bean stew, drop into the pan half a lemon or lemon juice while boiling, as it helps remove toxins from the beans. Sauté the onions, herbs, coriander, celery and garlic in a frying pan, then add the tomato paste. Make sure to sauté the ingredients well enough to eliminate the tomato flavour. Pour the mixture into a bean pot and stir well. You can use a potato masher if you want a smoother mix. The dish should ideally have an almost soup-like consistency. Add salt and pepper to taste and serve with gluten-free bread of your choice, chili, or hot Mchadi. Imeretians don't use tomato paste, so you can also easily make a non-tomato option.

BLENDED LOBIO WITH ALMONDS

HOW TO MAKE

When the beans of your choice are boiled, drain them well. Use the food processor to mix the ground almonds, garlic, onion and dry herbs first, then mix with the drained beans.

Add vinegar to taste and toss it well. Decorate with pomegranate seeds or herbs.

INGREDIENTS:

500 gr beans

1 or 2 cups of ground almonds

1 onion

1 tsp of dried calendula, mixed with dry coriander

1 bunch of fresh herbs, such as parsley or coriander

Salt, pepper and vinegar to taste

1 cup of pomegranate seeds to garnish

    No Georgian meal is complete without the main condiments, among them Tkemali (plum or greengage, Ajika, and chili paste), dips or walnut sauce. Georgians serve these with any dish, be it meat, vegetables or just bread or cornbread. The uniqueness of these sauces is that they don't dilute or spoil the original meat or vegetable flavours. On the contrary, they enhance them. Best made in-season, they are easy to prepare and guaranteed to delight your guests.
    I love making Tkemali sauce. I found that large sweet plums are not suitable, but some red plums are okay if smaller and slightly sour. Greengages are rarely seen abroad, while in Georgia, they are widely available from May until August.
    This is a perfect addition to any fish dish. Chop the fresh coriander, crush the garlic and mix all the ingredients with watered-down vinegar. Pour over the fish slices or serve separately.

CONDIMENTS

HOW TO MAKE

Boil the fruit in a large, heavy pan. Simmer until the plums start to peel and soften. Tip the plums into a large steel strainer placed over a large bowl or pan - the pan can be used to re-boil the juices -and leave them to drain and cool.

In my family, we used our hands to squeeze the cooled plums through the strainer: as kids, we loved to get our hands in that squidgy mess, but a wooden spoon works just as well to crush the plums. Once you have only the stones left, put the plum juice over a low heat and leave it to simmer.

Meanwhile, blend the remaining ingredients in a food processor. Then add the mix to the plums and continue to simmer for another 10 minutes. Taste the mixture. If you feel it is too sweet or sour, balance it with salt or sugar.

The Tkemali can be kept in the fridge for up to 10 days. In Georgia, we make Tkemali to store in a dry, dark and cool place for the whole winter. Bottle lids must be secure, and the mixture needs to be re-boiled before storing.

INGREDIENTS:

3 kg red plums or damsons
5 bunches of coriander
3 bunches of dill
10 cloves of garlic
Salt to taste

RED TKEMALI

INGREDIENTS:

3 kg of greengages
5 bunches of coriander
3 bunches of dill
10 cloves of garlic
Salt to taste

GREEN TKEMALI

HOW TO MAKE

I love making this sauce. When abroad, I've found that large sweet plums are not quite suitable, but some of the red plum varieties, smaller in size and slightly sour, are fine to use. The availability of greengages varies. For example, in Georgia, they are available from May until August, while I only found them in the UK during August.

Boil the fruits in a large, heavy pan. Simmer until the plums start to peel, which shows they have softened enough. Then pour them into a large steel strainer over a large bowl or pan (which can be used again to boil the juices) and leave them to drain and cool.

In my family, we used our hands to squeeze the cooled plums through the strainer, especially as kids, when we loved the mess, but a wooden spoon will work just as well. Once only the stones are left in the strainer, place the plums and juice over a low heat and leave to simmer.

Meanwhile, blend the remaining ingredients in the food processor. Combine with the plums and continue to simmer for another 10 minutes. Taste the mixture - if you feel it needs more salt or it's too sour, balance it with sugar or salt.

NIORTSKALI

The essence of this sauce is that it serves as a perfect flavour to augment any dish which has been fried or boiled. I use it, for example, to enliven a dish of fish, beetroot and fried chicken.

Mix 20g of white grape vinegar per kilo of fish with fresh bunches of coriander and crushed garlic water.

INGREDIENTS:

5 cloves of garlic
200 ml of boiled water

HOW TO MAKE

Crush the garlic and mix it well with the pre-boiled water. When you fry vegetables and spices, use the leftover cooking oil and some fried pieces that got stuck to the pan. It will give the garlic water a better texture.

BLACKBERRY SAUCE

INGREDIENTS:

500g blackberries
Small bunch of fresh coriander
2-3 cloves of garlic
Salt, pepper and chili to taste

HOW TO MAKE

Crush the soft, well-ripened blackberries; use a sieve if you like. Then mix all the other remaining ingredients in a blender and add them to the blackberry sauce.

This sauce is ideal when poured over all kinds of fish and vegetables.

AJIKA GREEN SAUCE

INGREDIENTS:

- 300g green, hot chilies
- 50g garlic
- Coriander, parsley
- 70g + 50g dry coriander seeds
- A small bunch of fresh celery, spring onions
- 50g leeks
- 30g salt
- Mint leaves
- Some crushed walnuts can be added if desired to give texture

HOW TO MAKE

All the ingredients should be blended or put through a food processor, bar the mint and walnuts. You can, if you like, remove the seeds from the chilies.

Add salt according to taste, and, before serving, add some oil and the crushed walnuts.

This sauce will keep in the fridge for three weeks.

AJIKA RED SAUCE

INGREDIENTS:

- 300g red chili (possibly smoked for flavour)
- 70g blue fenugreek
- 30g coriander
- 10g savory
- 300g oil
- 150g salt
- 80g garlic

HOW TO MAKE

Make in the same way as the Green Ajika, but without the walnuts.

Georgian pastries, such as Khachapuri and Mchadi, are indeed the kings of the Georgian feast. Pastry Heaven is widely available in every corner of the country, and in each household you will taste them with a different texture, filling, or presentation. Remember, the key to a good Khachapuri is the love shown when making the dough, especially when it's gluten-free. Let's explore.

GEORGIAN PASTRY

LET'S BAKE

By far, this was the most difficult task. I've met several knowledgeable dough experts who do indeed make a mean Khachapuri and Georgian bread, but to make them gluten-free is another challenge altogether. Of course, you can use the gluten-free flour mix of your choice, or simply use the ready-made bread mix of the gluten-free brand you trust. That's what I did.

It is absolutely crucial to practice dough making. Get your kids involved, too: just like pizza making, making Georgian pastry is a lot of fun, especially for Khachapuris. Yummy!

Here are my recipes, my three most trusted options, which came out with success.

IMERETIAN KHACHAPURI

Different style Khachapuris are presented in every corner of Georgia in many variations and forms. 'Imeretian' Khachapuri is the most popular, made using pastry infused with yeast and white Imeretian salted cheese.

ADJARIAN KHACHAPURI

A boatshaped Khachapuri with cheese, butter and egg yolk in the middle, it is thought to originate from the Laz people, who were sailors. Khachapuri is a representation of the boat, sea and sun.

PKHVLOVANA

One of the most popular pastry fillings, widely consumed by all, including vegetarians and vegans. The pastry is purely water-based, and is filled with Georgian varieties of herbs and spices before being sautéed.

GURULI GVEZHELI

A crescent-shaped pastry filled with cheese and slices of boiled eggs, normally baked by all households to celebrate Christmas.

IMERULI KHACHAPURI
DOUGH OPTION 1

INGREDIENTS:

250g gluten-free flour mix
60g butter or lactose-free butter
1 cup lactose-free yoghurt or milk
1 tsp baking soda
1 egg or egg substitute
A little sugar or replacement of your choice, optional

HOW TO MAKE

This makes at least two good pieces of Khachapuri. First, mix the flour and butter well, making sure it doesn't end up with a rough sand consistency.

Mix the baking soda in a cup of yoghurt until it bubbles, and then add to the flour mix. Keep mixing by hand, as for small quantities of dough we don't need the bread mixer as we do for larger quantities.

Add an egg and keep mixing, adding salt and sugar. Sugar helps the Khachapuri dough to crust nicely. Use sunflower oil to oil up the dough. When you have a very soft dough, wrap it in clingfilm and put it into the fridge for about 20 minutes.

Once the dough is ready to roll, sprinkle plenty of flour on the table and get started. Normally, Khachapuri is made by flattening a circle of dough, then placing the cheese in the middle and gathering in the sides with your fingers. The sides are then tied in a knot over the cheese, and flattened again with the wooden roller. But since we're dealing with gluten-free dough, I consider this a hard task. I simply decided to make the Khachapuri by making the base and covering it, and the evenly spread cheese, with a kind of dome, connecting the sides by hand or fork. It worked well.

Cut a small line in the middle to allow the cheese to bubble out while in the oven. I used lactose-free cheese, mixed with egg or egg substitute. If the cheese is not salty enough, add some salt.

Bake for 12 to 15 minutes in a pre-heated oven at 200C. Spread the top with butter or lactose-free butter of your choice when done.

INGREDIENTS:

260g gluten-free universal flour mix
5g gluten-free yeast
1 cup lactose-free milk
1 egg or egg substitute
Salt and sugar replacement to taste
40g butter, melted

ADJARIAN KHACHAPURI
DOUGH OPTION 2

HOW TO MAKE

This version is also quite soft and is ideal for both the boat-style Khachapuri and the herb Khachapuri. Start by mixing the flour with the salt and sugar. Dilute the gluten-free yeast inside the milk and add to the mix. Stir, then add one egg if desired. Add the melted butter and put the dough in a warm place for about 30 minutes or so until it rises.

Roll the dough into oval shapes, and then fold in both sides. Secure the ends by sticking them together and open the fold by slightly pushing them apart, creating the boat-like shape.

Put some cheese inside and put it in a pre-heated oven at 180C. Baking will take 15 minutes, and then you will need to break an egg in the middle (optional) and continue to bake until the dough is crispy and brown. A knob of butter can be added before serving.

Pkhlovana, herb Khachapuri, is made simply by sautéing spinach, spring onions, and chard with oil and little bit of salt. Place the plants as a small ball in the middle of the flattened dough and pull the sides slightly inwards, leaving some herbs exposed in the center. Bake in a pre-heated oven at 180C for 12 minutes.

The Guruli "pie," which is traditionally made for Orthodox Christmas, represents the moon.

Georgian Khinkali making requires dedication, patience, and it can be quite daunting, but enjoyable if mastered correctly.

This was by far the most difficult dough to make. Try using gluten-free bread mix for this one.

INGREDIENTS:

250g gluten-free bread mix
5g gluten-free yeast
Sunflower oil
1 or 2 boiled eggs
400g lactose-free cheese mix

HOW TO MAKE

Simply make the yeasty dough or get yourself a pre-made gluten-free pizza dough. Flatten the dough and make crescent shapes.

Place the grated lactose-free cheese in the middle and add slices of boiled egg, at least 1 egg per pie, and fold it into a crescent form.

Bake in a pre-heated oven at 200C for 10 minutes. Brush with beaten egg if you like before serving.

See pic.on page 80?

*Xanthan gum is an important ingredient in gluten-free baking as it helps the baked goods hold together and develop elasticity (jobs normally performed by gluten). Like baking powder and baking soda, a small amount of xanthan gum is usually enough to do the trick

HARD-FLOUR DOUGH OPTION,
BEST FOR GURULI GVEZELI AND KHINKALI (SEE PAGE 82)

INGREDIENTS:

250g ready bread mix dough
1 kg mushrooms of your choice
2 onions
Clove of garlic
Salt and pepper to taste

HOW TO MAKE

First dice the mushrooms into small pieces and sauté with oil, salt, garlic and onions. Allow to cool.

Khinkali dough is a simple mix of cold water, flour and salt. The dough must be hard enough to roll and easy to manage when collecting the sides of the Khinkali during the making. Khinkali dough needs some serious work, and it's an excellent thing to do with your family-go on, give the kids a go!

ake a large pastry and roll it flat to around 1cm thickness. Take a medium-sized water glass and cut out circles. Flatten the circles down to 1 or 2 mm thickness. Place a spoonful of the prepared mushroom mix in the middle of each circle, collect the edges into a bunch, twist them, and press to secure. Ready Khinkalis should look like a small bulb; however, some flatten them, so choose your shape. Just make sure the juices don't run through.

Place the Khinkali in parboiled salty water and as the water boils, watch them rise to the surface. It will take at least 7 minutes.

Serve hot, sprinkled with pepper. They can also be fried when cooled.

Normally served with beef or lamb mince inside, I decided to opt for mushrooms. You could also try cheese or spinach.

MUSHROOM KHINKALI

Enjoy these Georgian sweets with Gurieli Georgian tea. Once again, the best Georgian brand of tea: Gurieli - Born in Georgia. Many thanks to Gurieli and its chief Mikheil Chkuaseli for continuing Georgia's tea history and for featuring in this book. Black tea, green tea and Meskhetian nettle tea perfectly complement all the recipes below.

SWEET TOOTH

This is a wonderful and quick pick-me-up dessert, originally made during the grape harvest season but which can be enjoyed all year-round with the help of gluten-free fruit juice alternatives.

INGREDIENTS:

3 liters sugar-free grape juice or gluten-free fresh juice
Cinnamon to taste
4 cups all-purpose flour

PELAMUSHI CUPS

HOW TO MAKE

Take a large saucepan and pour the juice in with the flour. Stir well. Heat the mix, stirring well, and let it simmer for 20 minutes. Stir regularly, so it doesn't stick to the pan.

You can use honey or agave syrup (or neither), and cinnamon to balance the taste. When the flour aroma disappears, consider the dessert done!

As an alternative to grape juice, high-dark berry juices would do just fine.

This is not very Georgian, apart from the topping of the grape juice Pelamushi, but still, to modernize the dessert and make it more palatable, I tried to create a sort of cheesecake base with gluten-free cookies, mixed with coconut oil or lactose-free butter. It's up to you. Both versions work fine for me - with or without the biscuit base!

INGREDIENTS:

3 cups (255g) gluten-free oats
1/2 cup (113g) light brown sugar or coconut sugar
2 tbsp honey
1 tsp ground cinnamon
1/4 tsp kosher salt
1/4 cup + 1 tablespoon olive or coconut oil
6 tbsp unsalted butter, melted (for a dairy-free option, try substituting vegan baking butter)

PELAMUSHI TORTI

HOW TO MAKE

Use gluten-free cookies of your choice or graham crackers. Try crushed gingersnaps, vanilla or chocolate sandwich cookies, biscotti, shortbread, vanilla cookies, even brownies, as long as they're gluten-free. I added some almonds to gluten-free crackers, and mixed them well with coconut oil and brown sugar (or no sugar; both work fine).

Lightly spread the crumbs into an even layer on the bottom of a springform pan. Using your fingers or the bottom of a measuring cup to press the crumbs into the bottom of the pan and up the sides.

Bake at 150-180C for up to 8 minutes. Let it cool completely before pouring on the Pelamushi topping.

Make Pelamushi as mentioned in the recipe above. Pour the hot mixture onto the crust and store it in the fridge. I added vegan gelatin to the Pelamushi mixture in this particular recipe to keep the structure steady. Decorate with dried or fresh fruits and nuts. Enjoy, and be ready to amaze your guests!

This is a true all-season delight. The trick here is to add a Georgian touch by stuffing the quinces with dry fruits, agave syrup and nuts. For the winter, you can use apples instead, equally popular in Georgia.

INGREDIENTS:

2 large quinces
2 tbsps agave syrup
Vegetable oil or butter
Dried fruits

HOW TO MAKE

Preheat the oven to 175 C

Core the quinces (or cut off the top half to scoop out the middle). Do not cut all the way through. Put in the agave syrup, butter, and finely chopped dried fruits of your choice.

Place them on a deep baking tray in shallow water.

Bake them in the preheated oven for 15 minutes, until tender.

Serves 2, or 4 if cut in half.

BAKED QUINCES WITH SUN-DRIED FRUITS

This super light but rich dessert is terrific for those wanting to impress guests or family who are over for dinner. Plus, it's a great way to use those lactose-free yoghurts

INGREDIENTS:

500g thick yoghurt
Cinnamon and cardamom to taste
2 tbsp chopped walnuts or almonds
2 1/4 teaspoons unflavored powdered vegan gelatin

LACTOSE-FREE YOGHURT WITH ALMONDS AND WALNUTS

HOW TO MAKE

It's up to you whether you want to use gelatin for this dessert. Mix together lactose-free yoghurt, some lactose-free cream, and pre-prepared gelatin. Place the mix in small dessert cups and chill overnight.

For the topping, mix nuts in honey in a small pan on a low heat, then add cinnamon and cardamom. Pour the mixture over the chilled yoghurt cups.

Alternatively, you can prepare Ghozinaki with 500g of walnuts, 500g of honey and a few spoonfuls of powdered sugar. The walnuts should be pre-roasted and then boiled in the preheated honey. The boiled mixture needs to be rolled flat on a wooden board and left to cool. You can then cut it into the shapes you like.

GLUTEN-FREE EASTER CAKE

The word "Paska" may not be a Georgian word, but it's as close to my heart and childhood flavours and memories as any staple Georgian food. My cousin Nino, who was a teenager when I was born, not only helped take care of me but also taught me many interesting tricks-of -he-trade on how to make this lovely Easter celebratory sweet bread. I remember my mum and grandmother colouring eggs* and baking non-stop: Paska was simply on every table, decorated with blood-red eggs. With or without raisins, Paska has changed over time and improved, and many bakeries these days add colorful dry fruits, glaze, or chocolates. I see no reason why gluten-free people shouldn't enjoy Paska too!

Nino, as many households in Georgia do, will make at least 20 large, medium or small Paskas at a time. I've cut down the ingredients to achieve the ideal measurements for 4 gluten and lactose-free Easter Paskas. Oh, and don't forget: Nino highly recommends pampering the dough with sweet words, to guarantee good spirits and a warm, love-filled room for Easter.

*Georgians love colouring eggs, but only blood red. Normally, they use the Rubia plant root, but to make our lives easy, simply use red onion skin, as much as possible, placed in a large pan with the eggs and boiled until the eggs reach your desired shade of red.

INGREDIENTS:

5 eggs

350g sugar substitute, such as stevia, monk fruit extract, coconut sugar or any of your choice

1½ kg all-purpose gluten-free mix

2 tbsp of gluten-free yeast

½ litre lactose-free milk or any vegan milk alternative and 250g of water

125g vegan butter

125g lactose-free butter

½ cup of oil of your choice

5g of vanilla

150g gluten free dried fruits of your choice, preferably currants, redcurrants or raisins

2tsp of each: ginger powder, cardamon and nutmeg.

*A mix of buckwheat flour, sorghum flour. Coconut flour, tapioca starch and xanthan gum can be also used.

For the glazing, use any gluten-free icing of your choice, or simply sprinkle with powdered sugar.

NINO'S PASKA IN A BUNDT

HOW TO MAKE

Start by mixing the yeast inside the pre-warmed milk. I find it works well, however you can start baking without it.

In a large mixing bowl, combine flour mix, yeast, 100g sugar choice and then start adding the milk and water. You can use a conventional bread mixer. Mix it well: you should be able to get a liquid consistency. Wrap the bowl in a warm towel and set aside. Leave it to rise for about 25 minutes or so. Now start mixing the egg whites, before slowly adding the yolks. Add the remaining sugar choice, spices, and vanilla, add the pre-melted butter and vegan butter. Add the mixture to the risen mix and add more flour if needed, with the cooking oil. Wrap the bowl in a warm towel again. Add the dried fruits before putting the dough inside the Bundt mold (or the mold of your choice). Nino keeps the dough in its mold for several hours and then bakes the cakes in a pre-heated oven at gas mark 150C for an hour, or until she confirms it's ready by poking it with the wooden stick. and seeing it come out clean.

Once the Paska is cool, start preparing the glaze. I love the recipe given to me by a local patisserie, made with vegetable shortening, fine salt, gluten-free powdered sugar substitute, coconut milk or any milk alternative of your choice, and vanilla. Simply mix all the ingredients together until you get the consistency you want.

*Nino pre-soaks the spices and dried fruits in alcohol, but this is optional, of course.

Ingredients for icing

1 cup vegetable shortening

1/2tsp fine salt

4 cups gluten-free powdered sugar replacement

6 tbsp vegan milk of your choice

A pinch of vanilla

An Easter lamb cake mold is not an easy item to get. For some families, it's like an heirloom. If you're able to get the original cast iron version, that's great, or look for a modern silicon mold of any shape.

INGREDIENTS:

2 cups sugar or sweetener
600g gluten-free flour mix
5 eggs or egg substitute
500 g lactose-free milk or yoghurt (yoghurt is best)
1 tsp baking soda
250g lactose-free margarine
1 lemon rind, grated
Cinnamon to taste

EASTER LAMB CAKE

HOW TO MAKE

Start by beating the eggs and sugar well with a mixer. You can use an egg substitute with the same success; both versions work just fine.

Slowly add the pre-melted butter or margarine and mix. Set aside.

Put 1 tsp of bicarbonate soda in the lactose-free yoghurt or milk jar and let the yoghurt bubble. Add to the eggs, sugar and butter.

Mix, slowly adding cinnamon and grated lemon rind or lemon essence.

Slowly add flour to the mix until you get a soft and slightly runny textured mixture.

Preheat the oven to 200C and prepare the lamb-shaped mold. I use an heirloom passed down from my friends grandmother, and I have seen them for sale in various places. Alternatively, use any silicon mold you like.

Pre-oil the mold with margarine or butter. Pour the mixture in with the lamb nose shape first, so the nose can be baked. Place it in the oven for 25 minutes and then take it out, turn it over, and bake for a further 25 minutes. Take out the baked lamb and stand aside to cool. Sprinkle with powdered sugar or decorate with a ribbon around the lamb's neck. Enjoy!

About the author: Helena Bedwell, a veteran journalist with 25 years' experience, works in many different countries, but she shares most of her time between Norfolk in the UK and Tbilisi, Georgia.

'Gluten-Free and Lacto-Free Recipes from Helena' is her third book after 'Eat Georgian, Feel Good: Vegan and Vegetarian Recipes from Helena' and 'Georgian Flavours from Helena.'

17. FIRST COURSES AND LIGHT DISHES **25.** HEARTY SALADS **31.** HOT STARTERS **37.** HOT DISHES ON KETSI **43.** SOUPS **47.** MAINS **63.** BEANS **67.** CONDIMENTS **73.** GEORGIAN PASTRY **85.** SWEET TOOTH

Made in the USA
Monee, IL
04 May 2026

49442171R00064